Changing You!

A GUIDE TO Body Changes and Sexuality

Dr. Gail Saltz

illustrated by

Lynne Avril Cravath

PUFFIN BOOKS

For Natalie Dolgov and Anita Saltz: genuine,
loving women of great spirit who are very special to me
—G.S.

PUFFIN BOOKS
Published by the Penguin Group
Penguin Young Readers Group, 345 Hudson Street, New York, New York 10014, U.S.A.
Penguin Group (Canada), 90 Eglinton Avenue East, Suite 700, Toronto, Ontario, Canada M4P 2Y3
(a division of Pearson Penguin Canada Inc.)
Penguin Books Ltd, 80 Strand, London WC2R ORL, England
Penguin Ireland, 25 St Stephen's Green, Dublin 2, Ireland (a division of Penguin Books Ltd)
Penguin Group (Australia), 250 Camberwell Road, Camberwell, Victoria 3124, Australia
(a division of Pearson Australia Group Pty Ltd)
Penguin Books India Pvt Ltd, 11 Community Centre, Panchsheel Park, New Delhi - 110 017, India
Penguin Group (NZ), 67 Apollo Drive, Rosedale, North Shore 0632, New Zealand
(a division of Pearson New Zealand Ltd)
Penguin Books (South Africa) (Pty) Ltd, 24 Sturdee Avenue, Rosebank, Johannesburg 2196, South Africa

Registered Offices: Penguin Books Ltd, 80 Strand, London WC2R ORL, England

First published in the United States of America by Dutton Children's Books,
a division of Penguin Young Readers Group, 2007
Published by Puffin Books, a division of Penguin Young Readers Group, 2009

1 3 5 7 9 10 8 6 4 2

THE LIBRARY OF CONGRESS HAS CATALOGED THE DUTTON CHILDREN'S BOOKS EDITION AS FOLLOWS:
Saltz, Gail.
Changing you : a guide to body changes and sexuality / Gail Saltz; illustrated by Lynne Avril Cravath.
p. cm.
ISBN: 978-0-525-47817-1 (hc)
1. Puberty—Juvenile literature. 2. Sex instruction for children—Juvenile literature.
I. Avril, Lynne, date, ill. II. Title.
RJ144.C4553 2007 612.6 61—dc22 2006035593

Puffin Books ISBN 978-0-14-241479-8

Printed in China

Designed by Irene Vandervoort

Note to Parents

At some point in elementary school, probably around ages seven to ten, your child will want to have a more specific explanation of where babies come from. By now they know that the sperm is in Daddy and the egg in Mommy, so naturally they are wondering, "How does one get to the other?"

There are many ways your child may ask, so be open to their questions and try to pinpoint exactly what information they feel curious about. For example, if they ask what a tampon is, answer that question, but also be open to where the questioning is going, because it may be their way of asking about sex. Again the key here is to be open, honest, and not filled with obvious embarrassment.

Many parents put off having this discussion with their child because they feel embarrassed. DO NOT DELAY! This is your opportunity to establish yourself as the source of sexual information. If you wait, then your children will hear about sex from their peers and will likely get misinformation that will be difficult for you to correct. In addition, they will view their peers as the source of information in the future, rather than you. Take the opportunity to lay the groundwork for instilling some of your morals and values.

In addition to giving your children correct information, tell them when you feel is the right time to have sex with someone—for instance, "when you love someone very much" or "when you are married." What you say now has great impact. It is a time to set guidelines; it is not a time to be disapproving. Scaring them into not having sex can have a lasting effect on their sexuality, which you want to be healthy and positive so that one day it will become a vital part of any good marriage. For girls, it is important to tell them about menstruation and the body changes they can expect before girls in their class start menstruating. By age ten, there certainly will be one or two who are, and so the news will be out. It is very scary for a girl to enter puberty without any explanation of what is going on or reassurance that it is normal. If your daughter has not brought anything up by this time, you should initiate the conversation.

Hopefully, this book will be a useful tool to guide you through these very important conversations about sex.

Your body is amazing! It can do so many things—play, eat, read, run, swim, and sleep. It is constantly changing and growing, inside and out. Every day, you are getting taller, stronger, and bigger, too.

Do you ever wonder what all these changes mean? They mean that your body is getting ready so that one day, you can make a baby!

Sometime between the ages of nine to fourteen (it can be a little earlier or later), boys and girls enter a time called puberty. During puberty, your body changes and looks more and more like an adult's. But the changes happen gradually, and you really are still a kid. So, what does this feel like?

Well, sometimes this can feel confusing. You may feel excited and thrilled with the changes one day and then kind of grumpy and even scared the next. It's all very new, and it's all very normal. Most kids feel a little bit of everything. And everyone goes through the same physical changes. What kind of changes are they?

When boys enter puberty, their bodies grow, and their genitals grow, too.

If you are a boy, your genitals include a penis and, below that, a scrotum, the sac that holds two testicles. Also, inside the body, boys have glands called seminal vesicles and a prostate gland, which produce fluids for sperm to live in.

Penis

Outside View

Scrotum

Inside

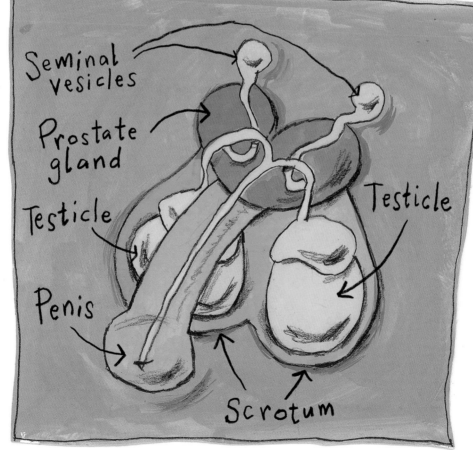

Seminal vesicles

Prostate gland

Testicle

Penis

Testicle

Scrotum

C L O S E — U P   V I E W

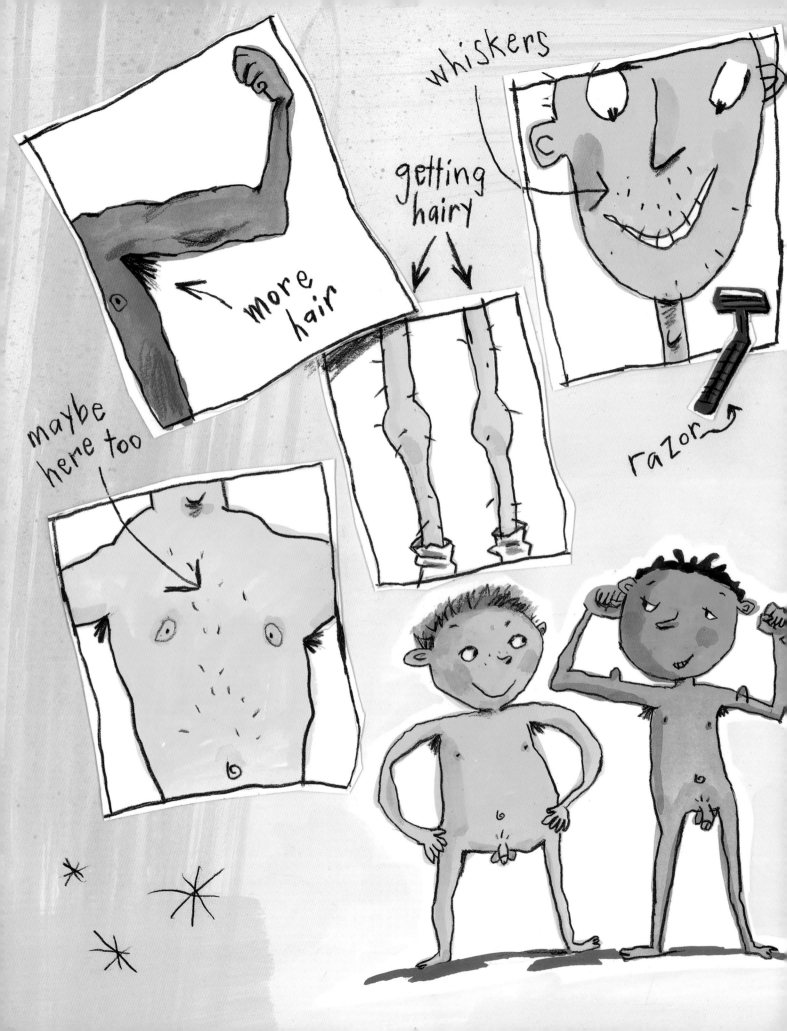

Jock STRAP good idea for sports days

Some mornings, it's not just the sun that rises...

In boys, hair begins to grow around the penis, under the arms, and over other parts of the body and the lower face. Their testicles begin to make sperm.

Sperm swim inside fluid that the glands produce.

Boys will also have more frequent erections. An erection is when blood flow to the penis increases and the penis grows hard and stands out straight. This is normal, and the penis will gradually go back to being the way it was.

Girls' bodies are different from boys' bodies in many ways. Girls have a vulva on the outside of their bodies and a uterus and ovaries on the inside.

Vulva

Outside

View

The vulva consists of two sets of labia (inner and outer), a clitoris, and a vagina. The outer labia look like a pair of skin folds that cover the vagina and clitoris. The clitoris is a pea-sized bump toward the front of the vulva that is very sensitive to touch. The vagina is a stretchy tube that reaches farther back into the body; the uterus is attached inside.

inside

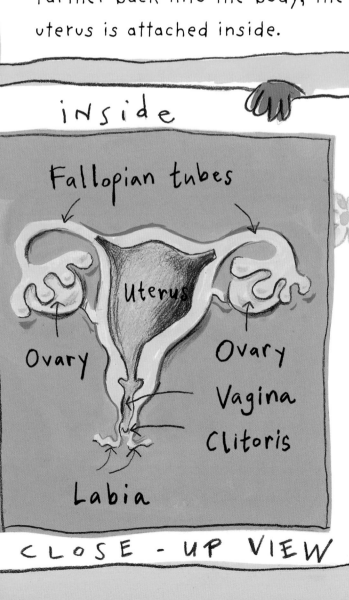

Fallopian tubes

Uterus

Ovary

Ovary

Vagina

Clitoris

Labia

CLOSE - UP VIEW

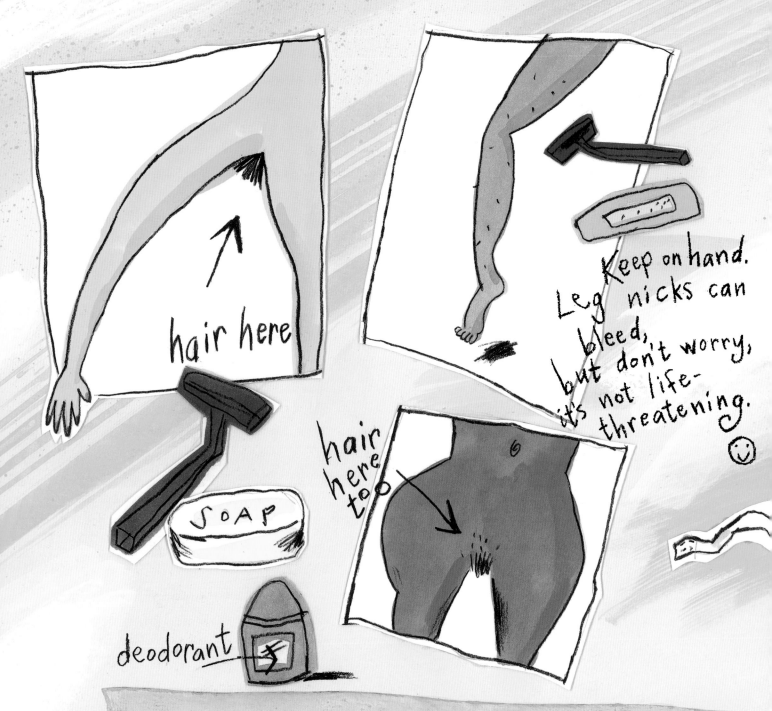

Girls' bodies grow during puberty, too. As with boys, hair will grow under their arms, on their legs, and over the outside of their genitals, particularly the mons, the triangle of soft tissue that covers the pubic bone. They will also begin to grow breasts. Sometimes breasts grow quickly, sometimes slowly, and sometimes one breast can grow a little faster than the other.

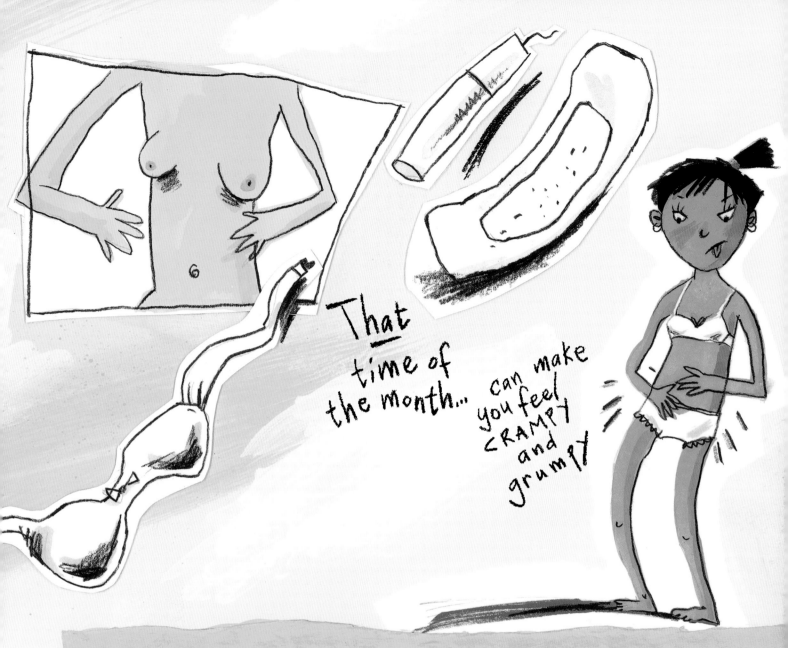

That time of the month... can make you feel CRAMPY and grumpy

The ovaries in a girl's body contain tiny eggs, which are released, one per month, into the uterus. About one year to eighteen months after their breasts start to grow, girls will begin to menstruate. Menstruating, also called getting your period, is when a small amount of blood and tissue that was lining the uterus is shed out of the body through the vagina. Periods happen once every month and last a few days. They are Mother Nature's way of cleaning the uterus when there is no baby inside.

Once a boy and a girl have gone through all their body changes, their sperm and egg are capable of making a baby. A baby grows when an egg and a sperm join together.

Since an egg is inside a woman's body and a sperm is inside a man's, you may be wondering, how does the sperm get to the egg? Good question!

When a man and a woman love each other and decide
that they want to have a child, they will do something called
"sexual intercourse" or "having sex." This is when the man
lies very close to the woman and puts his erect penis inside
her vagina. It feels good for both the man and woman. They
will also hug and kiss and cuddle. This is a very special way
of expressing how much they love each other.

When this happens, the man's sperm is released through the penis and into the vagina. Thousands of sperm swim up the vagina, into the uterus, and toward the egg. If a sperm finds an egg, then it will join with the egg. This now becomes what is called a cell, and this cell will divide. Dividing is the way that it grows, eventually becoming a fetus, the word for a baby when it is still inside the uterus.

When a woman has a fetus growing inside her uterus, she is called pregnant. While the baby is inside the uterus, it will get all its food and air from its mother through a tube that connects them. This tube is called the umbilical cord. The baby will grow for about nine months.

Once the baby is ready to be born, the mother's uterus, which is made mostly of muscle, will begin squeezing the baby out. This is called labor. You may be wondering, how does a whole baby get out of a mother's body? Even thinking about it may seem a little scary. The baby will come out the vagina, which becomes very, very stretchy so that the baby can fit through without harming the mother. A doctor will help the baby come out of the vagina. After the baby is born, the vagina will go back to its original size and shape. It will be the same as it was before the baby was born.

After the baby is born, the umbilical cord, which attached the baby to the inside of the mother, is cut. Now the baby needs to be fed from either a bottle or from the mother's breast, which makes and is filled with milk. Breasts do not make milk unless the woman has given birth to a baby. If she has, then breasts can make enough milk to feed the baby for many months.

Then...

Now...

Later...

It is amazing to realize that one day when you are an adult, your body will be grown up and be able to have babies. Until you are an adult and ready to make such important decisions about being sexual with someone and about having babies, it is okay to appreciate and explore your own body. It is also good to ask questions about your body when you don't understand some change or when you feel worried about something.

Your body is such an important and special part of who you are. It can experience all kinds of wonderful, amazing things. It feels wonderful to be hugged by people you love. It also feels good and is perfectly normal to touch your own body privately. Remember, though, that your body is only for you to touch, and someone else's body is only for them. Until you are grown up and are with another grown-up who gives you their permission, your body and others' should stay private. If someone else ever pressures you about touching your body, you should tell them no and then tell an adult you trust.

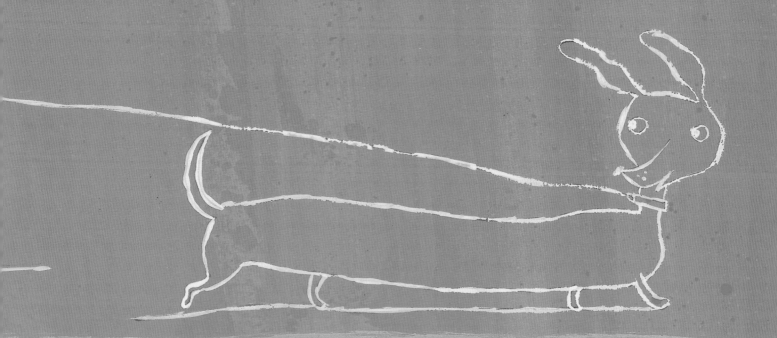

Sometimes as you are growing up, especially when your body starts to really change, you may think about "sexy stuff" and wonder, is this okay? Not only is it okay, most kids do. Everybody's thoughts may be a little different, and you may feel you want to keep yours private. But if any thoughts you are having are ever worrying you or seem scary, it really helps to talk about it with someone like a parent.

So now you know how your body will change as you grow up. You also know how the sperm gets to the egg and where babies come from. It isn't really all that mysterious, but it is rather magical, because our bodies are pretty amazing and also do some very special things!

Here are some general guidelines to consider when preparing to talk to your child about sexuality.

1. Find out exactly what your child is asking about. Then provide them with honest and correct information. You do not need to give them sexual details that they are not specifically asking about. Let them guide the conversation.

2. If it makes you more comfortable, use a book as a tool.

3. Start the conversation by expressing your expectations. For example, you can say, "Sex is a way of expressing your love to your husband or wife someday." A recent study showed that a mother's opinion about sex definitely affected the age of their daughter's first sexual encounter.

4. If you are particularly anxious about sexual matters, be aware that your child may interpret your anxiety as a message that there is something shameful about sex. Prepare for your conversation by reading some nonfiction books written for preteens about sex. This will help to reduce your nervousness.

5. Before your child is in middle school, make sure you have this talk, even if they have not brought it up.